Other titles in the series:
The Crazy World of Birdwatching (by Peter Rigby)
The Crazy World of Golf (Mike Scott)
The Crazy World of Sailing (Peter Rigby)
The Crazy World of Sex (David Pye)
The Crazy World of Skiing (Craig Peterson & Jerry Emerson)

Published in Great Britain by Exley Publications Ltd,
16 Chalk Hill, Watford, Herts, United Kingdom WD1 4BN.

Distributed in the United States by Interbook,
14895 E. 14th Street, Suite 370, San Leandro, CA 94577, USA.

Printed and bound in Hungary.

British Library Cataloguing in Publication Data
Pye, David
The crazy world of jogging.
I. Title
741.5'942 NC1479

ISBN 1-85015-061-3

the CRAZY world of JOGGING

Cartoons by
David Pye

EXLEY

RELAX.
TRY
JOGGING

"He likes jogging but only during the breaks."

"I think Jason's had enough, Darling."

"No officer, it's not my little kitty this time."

"I'm not wearing a bra. What's your excuse?"

"Give it up Geoffrey … there's more to life than a place in The Guinness Book of Records."

"O K, the style's not much, but you have to admire his guts ..."

"Slow down Parkinson, you're making Ms Zuckermann's shorthand come out wobbly."

"Well, I reckon a 30-pound dog fastened to one leg for 3 miles, must be worth at least 10 seconds ..."

"I can still hear footsteps, Guy!"

"Not bad – seven bars in nine minutes, ten seconds ..."

"Here comes another lunatic. I wonder if he's got a sprint finish?"

"Why don't we go to my place and replace our lost body-juices?"

"Evenin' Ma'am. Does this belong to you? We found it wandering about, vowing to take up gardening."

"You're quite right, I don't look like a jogger.
That's because I'm a mugger!"

CIRCUS

"He must have 'Chariots of Fire' on his tape!"

"Teach him!"

"Yes, I do admire their nerve, but when they're that size they ought to pay an extra tax!"

"Glass of beer and an ambulance, Doreen."

"Watch out for the bollards!"

"Yes, I do admire their nerve, but when they're that size they ought to pay an extra tax!"

"Glass of beer and an ambulance, Doreen."

"Following wind? The only following wind I'm aware of is the result of your three helpings of baked beans!"

"Can't we skip it tonight? The rain will ruin my new tracksuit …"

"Caught you! One cheese sandwich equals five times around the block!"

"Now, there's a thought ... painting the average kitchen ceiling is equal to jogging only four miles!"

"Dad's sulking. Two boy scouts insisted on helping him across the road ..."

"Gotcha! I thought you were running twice around the park rather too quickly!"

"Dad's just passed through the pain barrier."

"Kev, try not to get all our best customers."

"I'm not saying you're out of condition, but the machine appears to be laughing!"

"Don't leave me ... Don't leave me!"

"Don? Something's come up and I can't make my 11am workout. Take 5 laps round the block for me."

"You can always spot the beginners. They can't resist store windows."

"GOAL!!! I got him again Mom!"

"You can always spot the beginners. They can't resist store windows."

"GOAL!!! I got him again Mom!"

"Gordon! Can you hear me?"

"I'm just going out for a couple of laps with the boys..."

"Well, that's two laps – anybody want a third?"

"That's it! You're putting your feet down much more delicately now."

"Gee, Barry – did you see the size of that bird?!"

"Compulsive jogging isn't unknown Mr Leapwell ... Mr Leapwell?"

"Well, looking at you, the term seems inappropriate, but you've got athlete's foot."

"The male of our species is stronger …"

"I can't stand show offs. I'd sock him one if I could only catch him!"

JOG
AND
LIVE
LONGER

GUARD DOG
LOOSE

"Been jogging, by any chance?"

"Knees up Sweetie! Only another five miles!"

"It's trying to breathe and hold my guts in when I see pretty girls that tires me out ..."

"That's pretty good. Tomorrow we'll start on the other leg ..."

I WONDER IF THERE'S ANYONE UP THERE, JOGGING ALONG WONDERING IF THERE'S ANYONE DOWN THERE JOGGING ALONG?

"And I want you in bed by the time Dad is back from his wobble – er – jog!"

"There goes young Janie Lovejoy – still very self-conscious but anyone can recognise that behind a mile away!"

"Scoutship to base … scoutship to base … it's some sort of religious ceremony. They put special clothes on, rush about round and round, fall down and mutter 'Oh God! Oh God!'!"

"'Course, it depends on what you mean by 'deep' …"

"Carrots! Jogging! Carrots! Jogging! Do you think it's <u>worth</u> trying to prolong our lives?"

"All the way to the corner and back? Wow!"

"O K! Sound effects! Car coming!"

"Yes, well, I'm older than you and I say we should change our route …"

"Will our insurance company class Mr Piggott as an act of God?"

"I know it's supposed to be the equivalent of a two-mile run, but there's no need to dress for the part!"

"Cheat! It was my turn to trip one up!"

CASEY'S
BALL
BEARINGS

POSE SPORT
NEW
PLATFORM TRAINERS FOR THE SHORTER RUNNER
VERRUKA SWEAT TOP £500·00

SCRUMMY
ICE CREAM

"You jog and I alter your bloody clothes. Why can't you be nice and fat like you used to be!"

"Hmm – brand new outfit … going like a train … Do you remember when we were beginners?"

"There now, you back me up when I tell Dad he jogs in his sleep!"

"You may feel more comfortable. I <u>don't</u>!"

SUPERGRIP
RUNNING
SHOES

"Good morning. I'm from the Consumer Report team. I'd like a word with you about certain promises made to Mr Pratt here."

"Doesn't this sort of damage you?"

"Glasses? Normally, yes, but they steam up when they're jogging ..."

"It was an absolute scream .. he came rushing in shouting, 'Ten minutes to Macdonald's and back's not bad for a novice!', fell over the cat and broke his leg!"

"I know they were expensive, but you can't keep plastic bags on them forever ..."

Dunjoggin

Other books in the 'Crazy World' series:

The Crazy World of Sex, £3.95; $6.95. Also by David Pye. A light-hearted look at the absurdities and weaker moments of human passion. Very funny and in (reasonably) good taste.

The Crazy World of Birdwatching, £3.95; $6.95. By Peter Rigby. Over eighty cartoons on the strange antics of the twitcher brigade. One of our most popular pastimes, this will be a natural gift for any birdwatcher.

The Crazy World of Golf, £3.95; $6.95. By Mike Scott. A perfect gift-book for golfers. Over eighty cartoons on the absurdities of the sport and the odd habits of those who take part.

The Crazy World of Sailing, £3.95; $6.95. By Peter Rigby. The ideal gift-book for anyone who messes about in boats, who has gone green in a storm or been stuck in the doldrums.

The Crazy World of Skiing, £3.95; $6.95. By Craig Peterson and Jerry Emersom. Over 80 hilarious skiing cartoons covering almost every possible and impossible experience on the slopes. The ideal gift-book for Christmas and for those with broken bones or a glint of fanaticism in their eyes. 'A riotous suggestion … very funny and very original.' (The Good Book Guide).

United States
Distributed to bookstores by Interbook, 14895 E. 14th Street, Suite 370, San Leandro, CA 94577, U.S.A.

United Kingdom
These books make super presents. Order them from your local bookshop, or by post from Exley Publications, 16 Chalk Hill, Watford, Herts, WD1 4BN. (Please send 95p per book for postage and packing.)